The Battles Within.

Steve Roome

BookLeaf Publishing

Presentation by *BookLeaf Publishing*

Web: www.bookleafpub.com

E-mail: info@bookleafpub.com

ISBN: 9789357442039

First edition 2023

DEDICATION

To my wife Tracey, thank you for finding me.

PREFACE

These are my thoughts, my memories, my dark places. When I was most alone I stood with a thousand other damaged lonely souls.

My Peace

She whispered sweetly in my ear,
Her breath upon my face.
So calm it was those words to hear,
In such an awful place.

As the sun went down, and in crept dark,
I was stretched out on my bed.
I had not waited for the morning lark,
As by the dawn I'm dead.

That pure angel stayed by me,
As my wounds they sealed my fate.
Peace at last washed over me,
As I passed through heavens gate.

Can I ?

Can I go out to play please ?
  Yes, enjoy yourself...
Can I have a picnic in the park ?
  Yes, have a great day...
Can I visit my nan ?
  Yes, yes, please do...
Can I go to school?
  Yes, of course...
Can I not wash my hands again ?
  Yes, why bother...
Can I have my family stay with me ?
  Yes, the more the merrier...
Can we all go out together ?
  Yes replied the Reaper, you can all walk with me !

I Want to go Home

Today we were told of our Middle East Tour
  Already, I want to go home.

The flight is depressing, not a smile all the way
  I don't like flying from home.

Oppressive heat and biting bugs
  I miss the comforts of home!

A recce for insurgents, in the all encompassing night
  I want the safety of home!

Contact is made, a firefight ensues
  Where is my home?

Explosions, deafening, shaking the horizon
  I need to be home!

Ever closer, my weapon stinging the earth
  Please, please take me home!

Electric pains, race through my body
  So far from home

Pain has faded, along with my light
  I will never go home!

Shellness Fields

Over Shellness Fields
    I learned to fly
So they could send
    me off to war.
It was over Flanders Fields
    I gained my wings
And to walk the beach
    no more!

January 21

Are you feeling...
Professionally isolated
Lonely
Segregated
Emotionally shipwrecked
Marooned
Deserted
Socially hollow
Depressed
Low
Mental drudgery
Confused
Empty
Sinking feeling
Doom
Nothing ?
At least there is upbeat poetry
Oh wait...

Night Time

I hate the dark, carried by night
I close my eyes, until it is light.

I close them tight, and try to sleep
And wait for the sun, over the horizon to peep.

As the sun, it starts to rise
I yawn and stretch and open my eyes.

I stretch out tall upon my bed
I hate the night, I think I have said.

Broken Crayons

What was done, was not for valour
But a calling, to give our all
Broken crayons still colour

Into dunes, frightened men did pour
Some to rise again, others to silently fall
What was done, was not for valour

Through choking sand we had to claw
The proud Guards still marching tall
Broken crayons still colour

Onwards, onwards the incessant roar
Stinging AK hail as men stumble
What was done, was not for valour

Sand and heat, burning to my core
Nightmares and flashbacks are all I recall
Broken crayons still colour

You never fully return from your last tour
Slowly, slowly I will not fall
What was done, was not for valour
Broken crayons still colour

The Pointy End

"Don't hit the pointy end"
Was the advice down the phone
"Have you moved it at all?"
"Are you sure it's not a stone? "

"Listen lady" is my reply
"My nerves do not smell nice"
"My, Oh my" I hear her gasp
When I say I have hit it twice.

A shabby private walks up to me
His beret all a squiff
"Have you hit the pointy end"
He asks me with a sniff.

Laughing I told him
I had tried to clean the muck
So I hit it only once
And then again, just for luck.

"You did what?" he said to me
"You could have been blown to bits"
"I know that now" I cried
"Now stop giving me the. .....heebee geebees.

They closed the beach
To look at what I found
"Well done mate" they said to me
For leaving it in the ground.

They said that if I find another
That they always will attend
Unless I have already hit
The bloody pointy end

Jack

I cried today when I saw you
Even though it has been so many years
My emotions they took hold of me
And I could not hold back the tears.

In my arms I held you so briefly
Before I carried you to your bed
To lay you in your garden
For your eternal rest.

I feel I have been cheated
All the years you have been gone
Not a day has passed since then
When I do not think of you son.

One day we will be together
And maybe share a beer
And do all the things we couldn't
Through all the missing years.

Until tomorrow my sweet child
When St Peter calls me back
And we can walk at last together
Rest In Peace my son Jack.

Ice Cream

Ding a ling a ling
Ooh the ice cream van
"Mum, can I have an ice cream"
Silence
She isn't there
I know I will ask dad

"Dad, can I have an ice cream"
Again silence
He isn't there
I know I will ask my sister

"Oi"
"Sis"
"Can I have an ice cream"
That's odd
She didn't shout at me
She isn't there
I know I will ask my brother

"Ere"
"Bruv"
"Buy me an ice cream"
Weird
He hasn't hit me
He isn't there
I don't know what to do

Where is everyone
Who am i
Where am I
I am all alone
I hate being old.

Odd Socks

Where do all the odd socks go
When I put them in the wash
They all had partners, as far as I know
But today one single sock is lost.

Why do odd socks leave home
Are they not happy on my feet
Have they gone to visit Rome
I will ask them when next we meet

Where have all my odd socks gone
Have they gone to find their fame
Will they sing a famous song
So everyone knows their name

Are my socks upon the moon
Or floating around in space
I hope I find them very soon
I need them for a race

Are my socks upon the seas
Sailing with pirates so fierce
I think there is nothing so funny, if you please
Than a sock whose ear is pierced

Have my socks been crowned for a day
By monsters down the drain
When will they return, who can say
As down the drain they reign

I wish I had my odd socks back
Where else could they be
Perhaps they slipped down the cracks
Of the cushions on the settee

I wish I had my sock once more
I think I have already said
I will check behind the door
Oh look, it's under the bed !

By The Sea

I hear I can find freedom and peace
Down by the sea.

I can lose the stress, the pain, the anger
Down by the sea.

I want to walk just one more time
Down by the sea.

All my problems sorted as I walk deeper
Down by the sea.

Everything is cold on my lifeless body
Down by the sea.

Trained To Kill

Profound bleak drudge caked in icy chill
Enveloped in a claustrophobic fear
My heart thumping a race which I can not win
A noise sparks me to life
Alert to the task I have to do
Creeping low to the horizon
Eyes squinting in the dying light
Objective spotted in the dancing shadows
Stealth steals my breath as I ready myself
This is it, everything I have trained to do
Ready.......go...go....go
Mission accomplished I got the spider.

End

"You prayed for me this morning
So rest while I am near
Stay with me my child"
            Is whispered in my ear

I answered
        "when my duty called
            And it called me to obey
Please take me I am ready lord
To end my final day."

A Mouse

There is a mouse
I see him now and then
As I sit and watch him
He sometimes hides again
Other times he scurries
As my mind drifts lost in haze
At these times I know he is there
As the minutes fade to days
The first time that I saw him
Was when I came home from war
Now he is there beside me
And I see him more and more
One day when I look in the mirror
And the battle within is done
I no longer want to be a mouse
For I was born to be a lion

2020

January started with avidity and earnestness
and
ended still full of dreams and refinements but with intense abstractions.

February haunts the recesses of my memory
And
Haunted it with a chill and unearthly foreboding ending with unscrupulous contempt for the gravity we are plunged into as civility dies like flies

March a crystallised embodiment of the age of cynical and selfish hedonism abdurate and impenitent greed as humanity partakes with rapacity and plundering of vital provisions
Of these people I am left ashamed and speechless

April we are walking somewhat unsteadily like a blind man feeling his way as this nightmare melts like a cloud in the early silent summer heavens

May is yet to be confirmed !!

A Veteran

Children spitting at me
The constant abuse
As I walk, doing my job
Avoiding stones
Thrown by invisible assailants
A smile means they are plotting
No smile
It is already planned
Checking. Rechecking
Calling in the slightest abnormalities
A noise, I heard a noise
Why is he running?
Take cover. Don't run
Repeat
Check recheck
Check point is stress to bursting
Mirrors under cars
No one is who they say they are
I am not a racist
I am a patriot a veteran with severe flashbacks to two conflicts
One fair and green
The other hot and sandy
I detest fireworks
I always look for an exit when entering a room
I trust no one as no one is left
Some came home
Others....well they had no choice
I don't think all of me came home
Some locals etched their names on my heart
Others made their mark on my kevlar
I am not broken
I am fragile
I laugh I cry
Slowly but slowly
I try not to die
I have seen what shouldn't be seen
But I am still not racist
I am a patriot. A veteran.

Paranoia

I saw him staring right at me
As I glanced up from my chore
And as I look it seems to be
He stares back more and more

I told my mum but with no joy
About how it made me feel
All she said was "silly boy"
"It is not a great big deal"

My dad he said "don't be daft"
"It happens to us all"
Then he smiled and let out a laugh
Oh parents can be so cruel

So I looked once more and I was right
There he was again
It always gives me such a fright
That stare is driving me insane

It is so bad I am losing sleep
And I feel so far from perfection
It is so hard when you keep
Being so scared of your own reflection

"I"

I learn to cry
I learn to talk
I learn to crawl
I learn to walk
I learn to read
I learn to write
I learn to react
I learn to fight
I learn to love
I learn to hate
I learn of destruction
I learn how to create
I learn peace
I learn war
I have learnt too much
I can't take no more
I learn pain
I learn to cope
I learn to survive
I learn to hope
I have learned to take
I learned to give
I have learned so much
I have learned to live !

Lost

There is an old man
  Living down our street
His head bent low
  And slow shuffling feet
He looks so tired
  As he slowly ambles by
So deep in thought
  And sadness in his eye
His heart is lost
  In some foreign field
Where he saw many of his unit
  Shot injured and killed
Men like him
  Had but one life to give
For peace and freedom
  So others could live
For you and me
  That life they sacrifice
And those who came home
  Slowly dying twice.

Remember

Don't cry for me, as I March by
Cloaked in November sun.
But shed a tear for Tommy Boy
Some mother's long lost son.

He stood by me on Flanders Field
In trenches full of mud.
Poor Tommy he was shot and killed,
As the fields ran red with blood.

So cry with us, as we stand proud
To remember what our comrades done.
Join with us and sing 'Abide' out loud
For poor Tommy,
every mother's son.

www.ingramcontent.com/pod-product-compliance
Lightning Source LLC
Chambersburg PA
CBHW051720130826
49812CB00034B/1271
9789357442039